TYPHOON K

K-63968, K-63969, K-53949 & K-4386 MRAP Armoured Vehicles

HUGH HARKINS

Copyright © 2020 Hugh Harkins

All rights reserved.

ISBN: 1-903630-79-7
ISBN-13: 978-1-903630-79-2

TYPHOON K

K-63968, K-63969, K-53949 & K-4386 MRAP Armoured Vehicles

© Hugh Harkins 2020

Centurion Publishing
United Kingdom

ISBN 10: 1-903630-79-7
ISBN 13: 978-1-903630-79-2

This volume first published in 2020

The Author is identified as the copyright holder of this work under sections 77 and 78 of the Copyright Designs and Patents Act 1988

Cover design © Centurion Publishing & KDP

Page layout, concept and design © Centurion Publishing

All rights reserved. No part of this publication may be reproduced, stored in a retrieval system, transmitted in any form, or by any means, electronic, mechanical or photocopied, recorded or otherwise, without the written permission of the publisher

The publisher and author would like to thank all organisations and services for their assistance and contributions in the preparation of this volume:

Central Research Institute Burevestnik; Central Research Institute Volna; JSC Izhevsk Electromechanical Plant (Enterprise), Kupol; JSC NPO Elektromashina; JSC NPO High Precision Complexes (NPOVK); JSC Remdizel (Remdiesel); JSC Rosoboronexport; JSC Zid 'Plant, named after V.A. Degtyarev (formerly OJSC Zid and OJSC Kovrovsky); Kamaz (KamAZ); Ministry of Defence of the Russian Federation; Penza Research and Production [Development] enterprise, Rubin; Press Service of the Central Military District; Press Service of the Southern Military District; Press Service of the Western Military District; Property Relations Department of the Ministry of Defence of the Russian Federation; Rostec Corporation; Tulamashzavod Production Association & Harkins, H. (2017) 'Pantsir Missile/Gun Air Defence Complex', Centurion Publishing, United Kingdom

CITATION GUIDE: (CRI Burevestnik) Central Research Institute Burevestnik; (CRI Volna) Central Research Institute Volna; ((Izhevsk) JSC Izhevsk Electromechanical Plant (Enterprise), Kupol; (NPO Elektromashina) JSC NPO Elektromashina; (NPOVK) JSC NPO High Precision Complexes; (Remdizel) JSC Remdizel (Remdiesel); (Rosoboronexport) JSC Rosoboronexport; (Zid) JSC Zid 'Plant, named after V.A. Degtyarev; (MODRF) Ministry of Defence of the Russian Federation; Press Service of the Central Military District; Press Service of the Southern Military District; Press Service of the Western Military District; Property Relations Department of the Ministry of Defence of the Russian Federation; (Rostec) Rostec Corporation; (Tulamashzavod) Tulamashzavod Production Association & (Harkins, 2017) Harkins, H. (2017) 'Pantsir Missile/Gun Air Defence Complex', Centurion Publishing, United Kingdom

CONTENTS

Introduction vii

1 Typhoon K-63968, K-63969, K-53949 & K-4386   1

2 Glossary   78

INTRODUCTION

The Typhoon K (Тайфун К (Taifun K)) family of mine resistant ambush protected wheeled armoured vehicles began entering service with the ground forces of the Russian Federation in late 2013/early 2014. The Typhoon K series was developed as an integral element of the Russian Federation plans to modernise its armoured vehicle inventory in the period 2010-2020. There are four major variants of the Typhoon K – K-63968 & K-63969 built on a 6x6 chassis and K-53949 & K-4386 built on a 4x4 chassis. All variants can be armed with automatic combat modules, the 4x4 variants being outfitted with more diverse weapons options, ranging from medium/heavy machine guns and 30 mm automatic grenade launchers to 30 mm automatic gun armed uninhabited turrets for the K-4386. The K-53949 and K-4386 have been further developed as fire support vehicles armed with mortar complexes. The K-53949 has also been developed as a dedicated medical module (further developed into two distinct sub-variants) and for engineering (mine carrier) and command posts. The K-4386 has been further developed as the MTP-K tactical reconnaissance platform and as the Typhoon Air-Defence Vehicle for carriage of Igla-S surface to air missiles.

This volume adopts a free flowing style rather than the traditional chapter format, due to the interrelated relationship between the variants and weapon systems. The volume sets out to detail the Typhoon K genesis, design and initial entry into service with the ground forces of the Russian Federation. All technical data relating to the respective Typhoon K platforms, weapon systems and components have been furnished by the respective design bureaus, as has much of the imagery/graphics, with additional impute from the Ministry of Defense of the Russian Federation.

1

TYPHOON K-63968, K-63969, K-53949 & K-4386

The programs that emerged in 2010 as the Typhoon K (KamAZ) and Typhoon U (Ural) family of MRAP (Mine Resistant Ambush Protected) armoured vehicles was initially conceived in the Soviet Union of the early 1980's, apparently under the code-name 'Garage'. With the dissolution of the Soviet Union on 25 December 1991, all but the most crucial defence programs were put on hold or cancelled outright as the main successor state, the Russian Federation, struggled with a harsh post-Soviet economic downturn. It was not until 2010, with the release of documentation for the future concept for development of Russian armoured vehicles in the second decade of the twenty first century that the program was resurrected in earnest. The MODRF (Ministry of Defence of the Russian Federation) Minister for Defence authorised the Typhoon K family as part of the wider 'Concept for the development of Military Automotive Equipment of the Armed Forces of the Russian Federation for the period until 2020' (MODRF). This effectively kick-started development of several families of standardised armoured vehicles for the Russian ground forces and potential export.

Typhoon K/U research, design, development, build and testing, involved cooperation of around 120 partner enterprises (Remdizel). Following the 2010 authorisation, work proceeded rapidly as the Russian Federation embarked upon large-scale rearmament programs to replace outdated Soviet era equipment – the mainstay of her armoured forces. This rearmament was intended to field some 14,000 armoured vehicles, ranging from MBT (Main Battle Tank) (modernised and new), IFV (Infantry Fighting Vehicle) to MRAP vehicles (MODRF).

Typhoon K-63968 (16+2 – 16 passenger + 2 crew capacity) starboard and Typhoon K-63969 (10+2 capacity) port side. Rostec

The new generation of Russian MRAP vehicles are primarily designed, as was the case for western MRAP designs, for operations against irregular forces with limited offensive/defensive capabilities. This was a deviation from the previous Soviet practice of producing armoured vehicles suited first and foremost to large-scale mechanised warfare against a powerful enemy of considerable offensive and defensive capability. This was necessary during the Cold War era when the large-scale clash of armies on the European central front dominated defence planning of the power blocs of East and West. MRAP assets can be employed in various roles in armoured operations against fielded armies. The Typhoon K/U were designed on experience gained in conflicts that emanated from the break-up of the Soviet Union. The design teams would particularly draw on experience gained in the two Chechen wars of the mid-1990's through the early 2000's. Russian designers would also have examined NATO (North Atlantic Treaty Organisation) nations experiences in Afghanistan (from 2001) and Iraq (from 2003), where small-scale convoy ambush and IED (Improvised Explosive Device) were the major threats from limited capability insurgent forces fighting the occupations.

TYPHOON K

Typhoon K-53949 (top) and Typhoon K-4386 (bottom) 4x4 MRAP vehicles.
Rosoboronexport/Remdizel

Предназначен для перевозки личного состава, а также для установки различного целевого оборудования или систем вооружений.

Top: The Ural family of Typhoon K 6x6 vehicles (top) have a distinctly different exterior layout to the KamAZ Typhoon K vehicles, but all are built on the same unified platform. The accompanying Russian language text translates to English as more or less indicating role – transporting troops and for installation for targeting and weapon systems. Above: These Ural Typhoon U vehicles, equipped with external remote operated combat module, are operated by Russian ground forces. MODRF

At the heart of the Typhoon K/U concept, capable of operations at altitudes ranging from sea level to 4500 m above sea level, was provision of enhanced survivability against conventional mines and IED's. Extended ground clearance and a 'V' shaped vehicle bottom, designed to channel blast energy away from the vehicle (integral to all Typhoon K/U variants), were two of the design traits intended to enhance crew survivability. The extended ground clearance also increased the vehicles rough terrain capability (Remdizel).

The Typhoon K – K-63968, K-63969, K-53949 and K-4386 – and Typhoon U – Ural-63095 & Ural-63099 – families of armoured vehicles, although fundamentally different in their respective appearance, are developed on a single unified, modular, platform. There is another armoured vehicle referred to under the Typhoon nomenclature – the Typhoon M BDM, which is distinctly different in appearance to the Typhoon K/U platforms. This vehicle, in service with the Russian Federation Strategic Missile Forces, is based on the BTR-82/A wheeled armoured personnel carrier chassis and is intended to escort RS-24 Yars mobile nuclear armed intercontinental ballistic missile regiments on field deployment (Property Relations Department of the Ministry of Defence of the Russian Federation, 2018). The Typhoon M, despite being externally dissimilar, apparently incorporates advanced protection features developed for the Typhoon K/U.

Major advances in the Typhoon K design were conducted in 2011, the same year that the veil of absolute secrecy surrounding the program was lifted. This allowed development vehicles to be demonstrated at a Ministry of Defence of the Russian Federation research and test facility near Moscow. The classified nature of the program meant that development was conducted firmly behind closed doors, the next demonstration of a Typhoon K design being presented to the President of the Republic of Tatarstan, Russian Federation, in 2013. The following year (May 2014), a single Typhoon K took part in the Victory Day parade in Moscow, this being followed by participation of two Typhoon's, a K and U variant, at the Victory Day parade in Moscow on 9 May 2015 (Remdizel). Sharing much of the same design technology, the Typhoon K and Typhoon U developments were offered in direct competition with each other for Russian Federation ground forces contracts (Rostec).

As outlined above, there are four distinctly separate designs that carry the Typhoon K Designation – Typhoon K-63968, Typhoon K-63969, Typhoon K-53949 and the Typhoon K-4386, the latter designed for the Russian Federation Airborne Forces. The Typhoon K-53949 Medical Module, divided into two distinct configurations, is a sub-model of the K-53949. The K-63968 and the K-63969 are built on 6x6 wheel chassis whilst the K-53949, K-53949 Medical Module and K-4386 are built on a 4x4 chassis (Remdizel). The modular design allows the platforms to be used for many purposes, ranging from the basic passenger/cargo transport to direct battle support vehicles armed with various combat modules (Rostec).

There are design plans for a Typhoon K 8x8 chassis variant, but, as of December 2019, there is no indication that this has been brought to the hardware stage. In 2015, Rostec Corporation indicated that the 8x8 vehicles was being considered as a platform for the installation of Pantsir missile/gun short-range air defence systems (Rostec), currently integrated on Kamaz-6560 8x8 unarmoured chassis in Russian Federation Aerospace Forces and Naval terrestrial based air defence forces service (Harkins, 2017). The Remdizel built Tornado armoured chassis has also been demonstrated with the Pantsir complex installed in 2018, which, assuming it is successful in gaining a Russian domestic order for the Russian ground forces, may result in the proposed 8x8 variant of the Typhoon K being dropped.

The Typhoon K series was introduced to operate alongside a plethora of other wheeled armoured vehicles, including Tigr (4x4 armoured vehicle), which entered production in 2005. From 2015, Tigr M was extensively deployed to support Russian operations countering extremists groups in the Syrian Arab Republic where the vehicles often received projectile hits that caused only superficial damage to the armour body and or armoured glass. In Russian service Tigr M can be equipped with the Arbalet-DM combat module. Other potential weapon options include the Kornet-D1 ATGM (Anti-Tank Guided Missile) system.

The 6x6 vehicles of the Typhoon K-63968 were developed for deployment ahead of the K-53949 4x4 vehicles. From 2015, the Typhoon armoured vehicles would become familiar associations of the Russian ground forces, 30 Typhoon K-63968 having entered service in a trials capacity, followed by a further 30 deliveries several months later (MODRF & Remdizel).

Tigr M operating with Russian Military Police supporting operations against opposition forces in the Syrian Arab Republic (top) and Tigr derivative leading BTR armoured personnel carriers during a Victory Day Parade (bottom). MODRF

ТАЙФУН К-63968
ПОДВИЖНОСТЬ И МОЩНОСТЬ

TYPHOON K-63968 – The Typhoon K-63968 was designed to transport personnel/cargo to a combat zone as well as conduct counter insurgency type operations against an irregular enemy force. The vehicle is powered by a KamAZ 740.354-450 diesel fueled turbocharged engine with a power output of 450 hp. that provides for high performance whilst retaining a portion of power in reserve for emergency. The engine is located aft of the armoured crew cabin (Remdizel).

Typhoon K-63968 during trials. Remdizel.

Universal elevated armoured car – Typhoon K-63968. Designed for the transportation of personnel and integration of weapons. Russian language graphic detailing a few characteristics, such as engine power and troop capacity and a few weapons options – 7.62 mm medium machine gun and 12.7 mm heavy machine gun. MODRF

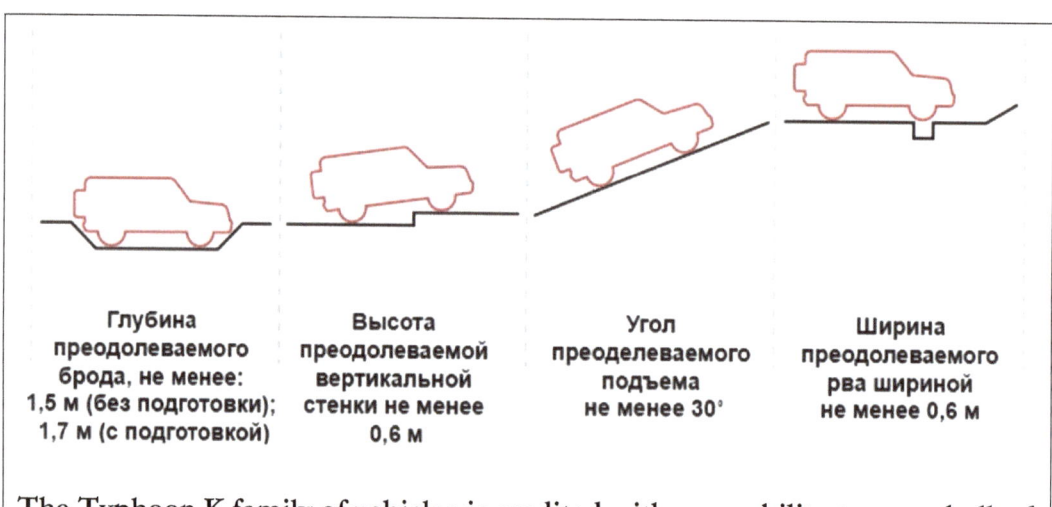

The Typhoon K family of vehicles is credited with a capability to cross bollard type obstacles of 1.5 m length without any preparation and 1.7 m length with prior preparation. The vehicles can navigate over vertical obstacles of 0.6 m with a climbing angle up to 30° and can cross obstacles, such as a ditch, with a width out to 0.6 m. Remdizel

The K-63968 design included excellent handling performance for rough terrain operations, through incorporation of a six-speed automatic transmission. The gearbox is a two-stage unit employing automatic differential lock. The design features a hydropneumatic independent suspension system that provides for vigorous alteration of rigidity characteristics and ground clearance (the latter feature enhancing blast survivability, noted above). The disc-brake mechanism incorporates an electronic anti-lock and anti-skid system (MODRF) and the tubeless tires, which feature adjustable air pressure, are designed for all-terrain travel (Remdizel). The tires incorporate blast guards and an auto inflate system (Press Service of the Southern Military District, 2013).

Although there will be variation between models, the Typhoon K family of vehicles are credited with a capability to cross bollard type obstacles of 1.5 m length without any preparation and 1.7 m length with prior preparation. The vehicles can navigate vertical obstacles of 0.6 m with a climbing angle up to 30° and can cross obstacles with a width up to 1.4 m (Remdizel).

Frontal-aspect view of a Typhoon K-63968 with the port side door to the crew cabin in the open position. MODRF

The Typhoon K family is protected by an outer layer of ceramic armour, beneath which is a liner of armoured steel. The vehicle is designed to function following a blast of up to 8 kg TNT equivalent explosive detonating underneath the vehicle body or beneath any of its wheels. MODRF

The ability to absorb damage from land mines and IED, and withstand ballistic impacts from low calibre direct fire weapons, was a primary design goal, the intention being to exceed STANAG-4569 governing armour protection ratings for NATO MRAP. The K-63968 is designed to withstand explosive blasts up to mine protection OTT Class 3 and protect against small arms and light artillery fire up to OTT Class 4 (Remdizel). The Typhoon K family is protected by an outer coat of ceramic armour, beneath which is a liner of armoured steel Osch. It is designed to continue operating following a blast of up to 8 kg TNT (Trinitrotoluene – a HE (High explosive) chemical formation) equivalent explosive detonating underneath the vehicle or beneath any of its wheels – the tires are stated to be explosion proof (certainly designed to allow continuance of wheel operation following significant blasts, such as those emanating from land mines) (Remdizel & MODRF). By contrast, the MaxxPro armoured vehicles, procured for certain NATO operators, is apparently protected against explosions up to 7 kg TNT equivalent. The Typhoon K concept incorporated an armoured bottom surface matting designed to protect the interior from shaped charge explosions, which direct a jet of energy at a specific point on the vehicle in order to maximise penetration potential (Remdizel).

Infographic released in 2015, just over a year after the Typhoon K-63968 entered service with the Russian ground forces. The Russian language data basically translates to specifications: full mass, 22 tons; curb mass, 18.5 tons; speed, 105 km/h; carrying capacity, 1.2 tons; crew and passengers, 1/16 (conflicting data from Remdizel confirms a crew of 2). Weapons options: PKT 7.62/54 mm machine gun; 12.7 mm heavy machine gun and AGS-30V automatic grenade launcher. MODRF

The armour protection features all aspect resistance against direct impacts of projectiles up to 14.5 mm calibre, including armour piercing bullets fired from sniper rifles, medium and heavy machine guns and ballistic shrapnel from artillery munitions. The vehicles side armour is designed to withstand the effects of a 152 mm HE shell exploding at a range of 25 m without any disabling damage. In trials, splinters from 152 mm HE shells exploded two metres from a Typhoon K-63968 caused superficial damage, with some splinters embedding in the outer skin, but failing to penetrate to the interior of the vehicle. The frontal armour of the K-63698 is able to withstand direct hits of 30 mm cannon projectiles (Press Service of the Central Military District, 2017).

The glazing protection of windows of the crew compartment and passenger cabin ports is stated to exceed that laid down in the MODRF requirement, being compliant with international standard class 6A. The glazing is designed to withstand a hit from a heavy calibre machine gun of KVPT 14.5 mm calibre type at a range of 200 m, with the projectile travelling at 911 m/s (Remdizel & Press Service of the Southern Military District, 2015). There are variations in the build of the K-63968 in regard to outer lines. Some vehicles are configured with two glazed ports on either side whilst others are operated without the ports.

The Typhoon K-63968 frontal armour is designed to protect against impacts by 30 mm cannon shells and the cabin glazing is resistant to ballistic impacts of projectiles up to 14.5 mm calibre. MODRF

The armoured passenger cabin, which, along with the crew cabin (for two crew (MODRF), is air conditioned and accommodates 16 seated passengers (Press Service of the Southern Military District, 2013). The seating for the passengers incorporates measures to absorb shock from blasts. The seats are anchored to the vehicle upper sections rather than the floor, providing for a more efficient and less dangerous absorption of energy (Remdizel), a far cry from Cold War era wheeled armoured personnel carriers, which from the authors experience was the Humber Pig and Avis Saracen, both of which left a lot to be desired in regard to occupant comfort. The passenger compartment has an exit at the rear with an electrohydraulic ramp, with a manual backup, to allow timely debussing of the embarked troops. Although the ramp is the standard entry and exit for the passengers, exit can also be effected through the roof mounted ports in an emergency, such as if the vehicle has been damaged. The roof hatches can also be used for other purposes, including use as firing ports for infantry personal weapons (MODRF & Remdizel). The crew compartment and passenger cabin are completely airtight (hermetically sealed) to facilitate continued operation when operating in an environment of smoke or chemical agents (MODRF).

The Typhoon K-63968 design has six roof mounted hatches that can be used to exit the vehicle in an emergency or for troops to fire personal weapons from within the vehicle. MODRF

Interior of the Typhoon K-63968 passenger compartment. Rostec /MODRF

The Typhoon K-63968 incorporates a system of self-extracting winch, capable of taking a load of 6.75 tons. Other miscellaneous equipment includes a towing complex and an integral fire extinguishing system (Remdizel). External situational awareness is enhanced through a battery of onboard cameras positioned around the vehicle exterior. This also allows the vehicle to be operated in the event of damage to the armoured windscreen obscuring forward vision from the crew cabin (MODRF & Remdizel).

The Typhoon K series is equipped with an information management/navigation complex, BIUS GALS-D1M. This complex, developed for incorporation on a number of Russian armoured vehicle designs, can be employed in stand-alone mode or linked with other complexes in other platforms. This can be accomplished autonomously or under operator control in environmental conditions of -40° to +55° centigrade. The complex, which meets the requirements of GOST RV 20.39.304-9, performs a number of functions, ranging from accurate navigation in all operational environments, course development and guidance, employment of weapons (where applicable) and electronic warfare. GALS-D1M monitors the status of onboard systems, informs of host vehicle diagnosed equipment malfunctions, monitors the operating function of the engine and alternates the vehicle suspension as required to clear obstacles of different heights (Press Service of the Southern Military District, 2013 & CRI Volna).

Typhoon K-63968. MODRF

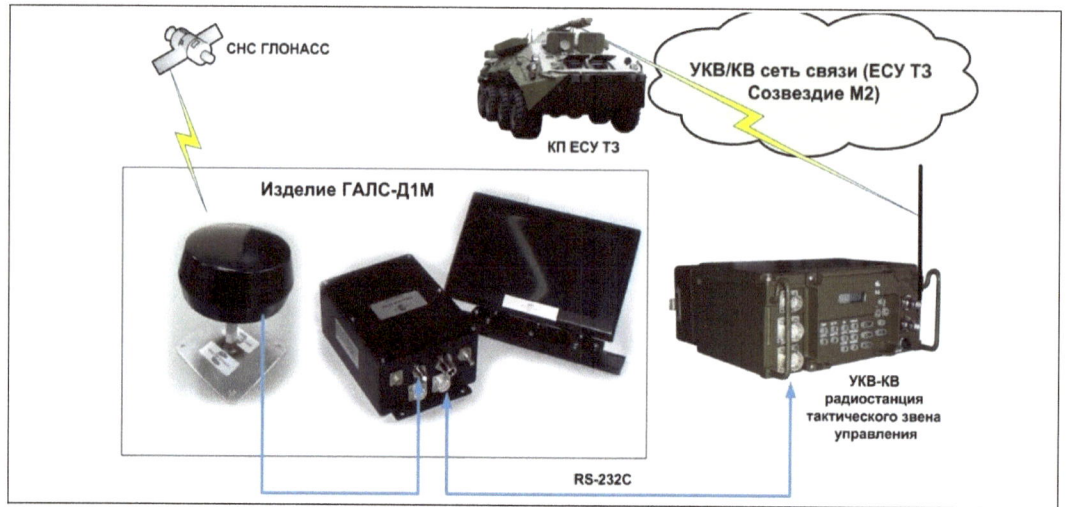

Graphic showing the process of GALS-D1M working with VHF radio station. English language translation of Russian language text in parenthesis: СНС ГЛОНАСС (SNS GLONASS); КП ЕСУ Т3 (KP ESU T3); HF communication network ESU T3 constellation M2; Изделие ГАЛС-Д1М (Product GALS-D1M); улв-кв радиостанция тактического звеча управлечия (ULV-KV tactical management radio station); RS-232C. CRI Volna

Selected components of the GALS-D1M (ГАЛС-Д1М). English language translation of Russian language text in parenthesis: Радарный блок дистанции (для заднего хода) (Radar distance unit (for reverse)); Цветная инфракрасная камера заднего вида (colour infrared rear camera); Устройство отображения (цветной монитор) (display device colour monitor); Радарный влок дистанции (distance radar lock); Центральный блок управления и навигации (central navigation and control unit); Режим дагностика (diagnostic mode); УКВ радиостанции (VHF radio stations). CRI Volna

GALS-D1M is composed of five major components: the central navigation system; onboard display(s); inertial navigation system; radar block unit (radar jamming system) and satellite navigation antenna. The complex consists of 1 central control navigation unit, 1 display screen, 1 inertial navigation system, 1 radar block system and 1 satellite navigation antenna. Operating modes include the ability to calculate the coordinates of adversary vehicles and weapons (such as artillery/mortar systems). Imagery of located adversary vehicles/weapons are then replicated on the GALS-D1M display unit with navigation data incorporated. The GALS-D1M can guide the host vehicle autonomously, the vehicles movement over the route from one point to another being recorded and stored in the system memory. Distance to and estimated time of travel to the designated destination is calculated with automatic display of various check-in points of a pre-determined route being displayed on the onboard navigation chart. Various points can be inputted into the system for future use. The system can automatically search for check-in points and various points designated as targets of interest, such as adversary vehicles or weapon positions that have been inputted. This can be accomplished by location, by coordinates or, for fixed building/street locations, by address. The system automatically displays relevant information in regard to vehicle speed, parameters of motion and direction of travel (CRI Volna). When operating in direct defence of the Russian Federation, the respective host vehicle GALS-D1M complex incorporates onboard electronic maps of all military districts in the country – Western, Northern, Southern, Eastern and Central – within the memory of the secure map, the information being replicated on the onboard display screen(s). Maps of areas the vehicles are deployed in, such as the Russian deployment to the Syrian Arab Republic from 2015, are uploaded as required. The systems integrated satellite navigation system automatically detects GPS (Global Positioning System) signals, such as those emanating from the Russian GLONASS (Globanaya Navigozionnaya Sputnikovaya Sistema (Global Navigation Satellite System)) satellite navigation constellation. The onboard secure radio communications complex, integrated with the GALS-D1M, operates in HF (High Frequency & VHF (Very High Frequency), the former frequency being used mainly when operating at tactical level within localised units (CRI Volna).

The GALS-D1M system is designed to operate in a hostile electronic warfare environment, whereby an adversary is actively attempting to suppress navigation systems. If GPS navigation is disrupted then the system falls back on the inertial navigation unit. This strapdown inertial navigation system employs microelectromechanical sensors, which are integrated with the receiver unit of the satellite navigation system and the GALS-D1M radar distance system (CRI Volna).

Typhoon K-63968 in service with the Russian ground forces (top) and during trials (bottom). MODRF/Remdizel

GALS-D1M characteristics/performance – data furnished by CRI Volna

Central Control and Navigation Unit
Power supply: 10-30 volts
Power consumption: 5 W
Dimensions: 167 x 127 x 127 mm
Weight: 1220 g
Operating temperature range: -40° to +55° centigrade
Central computer unit (with processor) frequency: MHz 800
GLONASS satellite navigation receiver, MHz L1 (CT/VT code) + L2 (CT/VT code)
GPS satellite navigation receiver, MHz L1 (C/A) code)
Satellite navigation receiver, channel numbers: 24
DISTANCE RADAR UNIT
Power output: up to 30 mW
Dimensions (diameter and length): 67 x 118 mm
Weight: up to 1,000 g
Operating range: MHz K-band
DISPLAY DEVICE
Resolution: 800 x 480 pixels
Screen size and type: 178 mm touch screen
Dimensions: 198 x 123 x 536 mm
Weight: up to 2,500 g
Operating temperature range: from -50° to +55° centigrade
GLONASS satellite navigation antenna
Frequency range: MHz 1574-1602
Gain (excluding cable loss): dB 32
Operating temperature range: from -50° to +55° centigrade
Weight: 500 g

K-63968 equipped with the Arbalet-DM combat module. Remdizel

Typhoon K-63968, K-63969 and K-53949 can be equipped with a remotely operated BMDU combat module, model TLMR 461114.001 Arbalet-DM (Crossbow-DM) developed by JSC NPO Elektromashina. This can be armed with either a 7.62/54 PKMB medium machine gun or a 12.7 mm NSVT or KOPD heavy machine gun (armed with B-32 API (Armour Piercing Incendiary), BZT-44M API tracer, and BS API) rounds as standard (CRI Burevestnik, MODRF & Remdizel). MODRF documentation states the module can also be armed with an AGS-30 automatic grenade launcher (Remdizel & MODRF), although this armament is not included in the documentation covering the export standard Arbalet-DM.

When Arbalet-DM is equipped with the remote controlled gun mount the weapon is controlled and aiming assisted through the host platforms onboard suite of five cameras that monitor the external environment (Press Service of the Southern Military District, 2013). Arbalet-DM can be equipped with a TV (Television) camera system, with a reported detection range out to 2500 m (daylight), a thermal aiming complex for the weapon, with a range out to 1500 m (low light/night), and a laser rangefinder complex. The module features an automatic reloading system and can track moving targets (including slow moving airborne targets, such as UAV (Uninhabited Air Vehicles), allowing accurate engagement whilst the vehicle is mobile or stationary. Prior to installation on Typhoon K, the Arbalet-DM was installed on the Tigr armoured vehicle (Rostec).

PKMB modernised 7.62 mm Kalashnikov medium machine gun. Rosoboronexport

The Kalashnikov PKMB 7.62/54 mm calibre medium machine gun can be employed on Typhoon K platforms and can be integrated as an integral element of the Arbalet-DM combat module. The weapon is fed 7.62/54 mm ammunition from a 250 round drum with non-disintegrating belt feed. Ammunition types include armour-piercing incendiary, tracer and increased penetration rounds (Rosoboronexport).

Kalashnikov PKMB 7.62/54 mm – data furnished by JSC Rosoboronexport & JSC Zid 'Plant, named after V.A. Degtyarev

Calibre: 7.62 mm
Cartridge: 7.62 mm x 54 mm
Belt feed capacity: 250 rounds
Rate of fire: 600-800 rpm
Normal effective rate of fire: up to 250 rpm
Muzzle velocity: 825 m/s
Sighting range for effective fire: up to 1500 m
Weight without mount: 7.5 kg
Weight including mount: 17.1 kg
Operating temperature rage: ±50° centigrade

Cord (Kord) 12.7 mm calibre heavy machine gun. Zid

Cord (Kord) 12.7 mm heavy machine gun for installing on 6U16 (Index 6P85) – data furnished by JSC Zid 'Plant, named after V.A. Degtyarev

Calibre: 12.7 mm
Round types: B-32 API (Armour Piercing Incendiary), BS API and BZT-44M (armour piercing incendiary-tracer)
Rate of fire: 600-750 rpm
Muzzle velocity: 820-850 m/s
Sighting range: out to about 2000 m
Technical resources: 10,000 rounds
Weight: (lacking sight and spares): no more than 60 kg
Length: 1980 mm
Height (horizontal position with sight): 550 mm
Height (horizontal position without sight): 500 mm
Width: 810 mm

The Typhoon K series of armoured vehicles can be armed with a 7.62 mm or 12.7 mm machine gun independent of the presence of a combat module as shown on a Typhoon K-4386 armed with a 12.7 mm Kord heavy machine gun, 2018. MODRF

The AGS-30 30 mm calibre automatic grenade launcher is specified for Typhoon K platforms (MODRF). This armament has good attributes in combating an enemy ambushing a vehicle convoy. As of 2019, it does not appear to be a standard armament for such vehicles, but is in widespread service on Tigr M armoured vehicles. The weapon can lay down suppression fire against dug-in personnel and those located on reverse slope terrain, out of line of fire for direct fire weapons, such as heavy machine guns and low calibre cannon.

The AGS-30 30 mm automatic grenade launcher (top) equips Russian Federation Tigr M armoured cars (above). On Tigr M AGS-30 is operated independent of the Arbalet-DM, this likely being the case with the Typhoon K variants (Typhoon K-63968 in background). MODRF

TYPHOON K

AGS-30 Automatic Grenade Launcher – data furnished by JSC Rosoboronexport

Dimensions (vehicle mounted) 143 x 132 x 837 mm
Calibre: 30 mm
Rounds: GPD-30, GPD-30UB, GPD-30I, VOG-30, VOG-17M, 7P36M and VSU-17
Firing mode: automatic
Muzzle velocity: around 183 m/s
Rate of fire: around 400 rpm
Weight: AGS-30 (without sighting system and ammunition storage box): 16.5 kg + 0.5 kg. Ammunition storage box empty weight, 2.9 kg
Sighting system: optical and iron. Can also be employed in radar sighting mode when applicable
Sighting range: up to 1700 m when employing VOG-30, VOG-17M, 7P36M and VSU-17 munitions and 2100 m when employing GPD-30, GPD-30UB and GPD-30I munitions
Radar sighting effective range: around 2 km against a human size target and around 4 km against a vehicle size target
Round weight: VOG-30 & GPD-30, 0.35 kg

Russian ground forces demining unit transported in Typhoon K-63968. MODRF

Top: Graphic depicting Typhoon K-63968 configured for Russian Federation Military Police operations. Such vehicles were deployed to support Russian operations in the Syrian Arab Republic against armed extremist groups from the second half of the 2010's. Above: Six Typhoon K-63968 vehicles in formation at a victory day parade. MODRF

There are two standards of Typhoon K exterior carrying the K-63968 prefix. The most common appears to incorporate the two external armoured glazed ports on each side of the passenger cabin (top) whilst the other omits these ports (bottom). MODRF/KamAZ

Page 30-31: Typhoon K/U and Tigr armoured vehicles can be equipped with a BMOZ combat module armed with a Cord (Kord) 12.7 mm heavy machine gun. NPO Elektromashina

A baseline combat module specified for the Typhoon K/U and Tigr armoured vehicles is the NPO Elektromashina developed BMOZ two-plane (horizontal and vertical)-stabilised remote controlled complex. This module is armed with a Cord 12.7 mm heavy machine gun with an ammunition capacity of 250 12.7 mm calibre rounds ready to fire and a total ammunition capacity of 1,000 rounds. Effectiveness of the armament is supported by the incorporation of a laser rangefinder, thermal imaging (for low light conditions) and TV (for daylight conditions) systems, gyroscopic sight and gun stabilisation system. The stabilisation allows for accurate firing of the weapon against moving targets out to a range of 1 km from platforms moving at speeds up to 20-30 km/h.

BMOZ combat module. NPO Elektromashina

MODRF documentation states that Typhoon K (model unstated) can be employed as a launch platform for UAV's (it is unclear if this is Orlan-10 (normally ground launched, or perhaps a smaller vehicle of the hand launched type, such as the TV-12 'Mosquito') and the vehicles are operated by specialist demining units (MODRF).

Typhoon K-63968 Tactical and Technical Characteristics – Remdizel & MODRF

Wheel formula: 6x6
Engine: Kamaz 740.354.450 V-8
Power, maximum: 331 kW (450 hp.)
Maximum engine torque: 1864 Nm (190 kgf)
Fuel type: diesel
Fuel tanks and capacity: two tanks, each holding 280 liters
Vehicle curb weight: 22000-26000 kg (Remdizel) and 18550 kg (MODRF). MODRF documentation also provides a value of 22250 kg for gross weight (below), the curb weight provided by Remdizel possibly referring to gross weight rather than curb weight
Vehicle gross weight: 22550 kg
Length: 8200 mm (MODRF) or 8266 mm (Remdizel)
Width: 2520 mm
Height: 2930 mm
Ground clearance: 463 mm (adjustable)
Angle of non-overcome lift by car: at least 60%
Personnel capacity: varies by role. 3+14 and 2+16 being most commonly quoted in primary source documentation
Transmission: automatic, hydromech with a 6-speed gearbox
Wheels: 10.00-20
Tires: 16.00 R20
Cruise range: at least 1000 km
Maximum speed: 105 km/h

TYPHOON K-63969 – The K-63969 has many design traits in common with the K-63968, but is distinctly different in other areas. It features the hydropneumatic independent suspension system, the self-extracting winch, capable of taking a load of 6.75 tons, and a host of other equipment incorporated in the K-63968 – towing complex, integral fire extinguishing system all-round camera system, communications, navigation and control complexes (Remdizel). The tubeless tires, the same as those incorporated in the K-63968, feature adjustable air pressure and are designed for all-terrain travel (Remdizel).

Typhoon K-63969. Remdizel

The lower capacity passenger cabin of the K-63969 can be accessed by the crew of driver and commander from their position in the forward crew compartment. This allows for onboard repairs to be conducted to elements of the power plant without exiting the vehicle, and allows the crew to exit through the rear hatchway, along with the embarked passengers. The K-63969 can be equipped with an electrohydraulic ramp, with a manual backup. When the ramp is in the closed position it is fixed in place by a system of two hydraulic locking mechanisms (Remdizel).

As is the case with the K-63968, incorporation of the model TLMR 461114.001 Arbalet-DM (Crossbow-DM) automatic weapons station on the vehicle upper section allows for all-round field of fire for independent operation, or in support of disembarked troops. The vehicle has different armour protection ratings compared with the K-63968. It is designed to withstand explosive blasts up to mine protection OTT Class 4 and protect against small arms and light artillery fire up to OTT Class 6 (Remdizel).

Typhoon K-63969 with the Arbalet-DM combat module and rooftop exit hatch for the crew compartment in the open position. Remdizel

Typhoon K-63969 vehicles during assembly, equipped with the Arbalet-DM combat module. Rostec

Three quarters rear-on and three quarters frontal aspect views of Typhoon K-63969. Rosoboronexport

Typhoon K-63969 Tactical and Technical Characteristics – data furnished by Remdizel with additional data from JSC Rosoboronexport

Wheel formula: 6x6
Engine: Kamaz 740.354.450 V-8
Engine power, maximum: 331 kW (450 hp.)
Maximum engine torque: 1864 Nm (190 kgf) (Rosoboronexport states 1900 kN and 190 kgf)
Fuel type: diesel
Fuel tanks and capacity: two tanks, one with a capacity of 400 litres and one with a capacity of 150 litres, for a total of 550 litres
Transmission: automatic
Suspension: independent
Vehicle curb weight: 24000 kg (Rosoboronexport states 23700 kg)
Vehicle gross weight: 26000 kg (Rosoboronexport states 27700 kg)
Power to weight ratio: 16.3
Load capacity: 4000 kg
Personnel capacity: 2 crew plus 10 passengers
Gross trailer weight: 8000 kg
Gross train (combined vehicle and trailer) weight: 35700 kg
Length: 7970 mm
Width: 2545 mm
Height: 3585 mm
Ground clearance: 430 mm (adjustable)
Transmission: automatic, hydromech with a 6-speed gearbox
Wheels: 10.00-20 (Rosoboronexport states 10.00-10)
Tires: 16.00 R20
Fording depth: 1.5 m (without preparation) or 1.75 m (with preparation)
Trench traverse: 0.6 m
Vertical obstacle overcome: 0.6 m
Gradient: 31°
Cruise range: at least 1000 km
Maximum speed: 105 km/h (Rosoboronexport states 100 km/h)
Electrical system voltage: 24 V

Typhoon K-63969 with Arbalet-DM combat module. Remdizel

Typhoon K-53949 armoured vehicle. Remdizel

TYPHOON K-53949 – The Typhoon K-53949 is the baseline model of the Typhoon-K 4x4 variants, developed to fulfill a variety of roles, ranging from passenger/cargo transport, field reconnaissance, battlefield casualty evacuation, to fire support with a variety of weapons options. The vehicles are designed to operate at altitudes ranging from sea level up to 4500 m (Remdizel).

TYPHOON K

Page 41-43: Typhoon K-53949 equipped with Arbalet-DM combat module. Remdizel

The K-53949 was developed primarily to reduce high acquisition costs associated with the K-63968 platform. The cost was further reduced by some 30% through substituting a spring suspension system for the more advanced hydropneumatic suspension system associated with the 6x6 Typhoon K platforms. The electronics suite was simplified as a cost measure and to increase the number of personnel that could operate same without requiring significant specialised training (Remdizel).

The K-53949 takes on a distinctly different appearance in the frontal, rear-on and lateral aspects when compared with the larger 6x6 Typhoon-K platforms. There are four side doors – two fore and two aft – with a further door/ramp at the rear for entry/exit of up to 10 passengers and crew. The afore noted independent spring-type suspension system enhances occupant comfort. This is designed to reduce the effects of vibrations on the occupants (Remdizel).

The K-53949 is endowed with the same level of mine/IED blast and small arms/artillery protection of OTT Class 3 and OTT Class 4 as specified for the K-63968. The protection suite includes tubeless tires, which feature adjustable air pressure and are designed for all-terrain travel. The K-53949 is equipped with a self-extracting winch, but with a load bearing of 8 tons – 1.25 tons higher than that available to the Typhoon K 6x6 platforms. Other equipment includes a communications suite, an all-round exterior view camera system and GALS-D1M information management complex associated with the K-63968 (Remdizel).

The K-53949 can be equipped with the Arbalet-DM model TLMR 461114.001 (Remdizel) or, the CRI Burevestnik developed 6S21 weapon station, which can be armed with machine guns of 12.7 or 7.62 mm calibre. Another option is the BMOZ remote controlled combat module armed with a Cord 12.7 mm heavy machine gun. The K-53949 has been mooted as a carrier for the Kornet-D1/M(EM) ATGM system. The vehicle mounted automatic launcher complex would typically be installed in two groups of four. The missiles are launched in a fire and forget mode against a number of target types – armoured vehicles and UAV or other slow moving air targets.

6S21 Weapon Station – data furnished by CRI Burevestnik

6S21 RCWS variant: 01
Armament: Kord (Cord) 12.7 mm machine gun
Ammunition belt capacity (ready to fire): up to 200 rounds
Maximum weight of station with armament and no ammunition: 230 kg
Elevation: -5° (can be increased to -15°) to +75°
Traverse: 360°
Elevation aiming speed: 0.03 to 40°/second (can be extended to 60°/second)
Traverse aiming speed: 0.03 to 40°/second (can be extended to 60°/second)
Remote cocking: available
Weapon stabilisation: not available
Sight unit: TV (Television) camera system plus laser range-finder with the option of enhancing the suite to TV/IR (Television/Infrared) camera plus laser range-finder
Dimensions
Height: 599 mm
Width: 850 mm (without ammunition box)
Diameter of module flange: 500 mm
Power consumption
Nominal: up to 0.8 kW
Short-time overload mode: up to 2.4 kW

> Kornet-M – data relates to export standard Kornet-E/EM, furnished by JSC Rosoboronexport
>
> Guidance: automatic
> Number of targets simultaneously engaged: 2
> Effective range: 150-10000 m for missile with HE (High Explosive) warhead and 150-8000 m for missile with HEAT (High Explosive Anti-Tank) warhead
> Armour penetration: 1100-1300 mm
> Ready to launch missiles: 8 (total missile capacity is 16)
> Operating temperature range: -20° to plus 60° centigrade

The K-53949 can be configured as a self-propelled mortar platform, armed with the 2S41 'Drok' 82 mm mortar system (Remdizel). Another K-53949 derivate concerns a planned intelligence gathering platform, which had not undergone testing as of late 2019. K-53949 vehicles were handed over to the 12th Main Directorate of the Ministry of Defence of the Russian Federation, effectively tasked with providing support to convoys transporting nuclear material. These vehicles, apparently procured to protect convoys of nuclear weapons systems in transit and at the site of deployment, may be the K-53949 lacking significant modification.

The K-53949 can be air transported by Ilyushin Il-76 and Antonov An-124 four jet transport aircraft as well as the Russian Helicopters Mi-26 heavy transport helicopter (Remdizel).

The 6S21 combat module can be armed with machine guns of 12.7 or 7.62 mm calibre. The baseline version is model 01 (page 45 and page 46 top), whilst model 02 (above) adds a laser range-finder unit to the TV sighting complex. CRI Burevestnik

TYPHOON K

Kornet-M ATGM system mounted on non-Typhoon K MRAP complexes. NPOVK/MODRF

Typhoon K-53949 4x4 MRAP during trials (top) and in service with a unit of the Southern Military District, 28 May 2018 (bottom). Remdizel/MODRF

Typhoon K-53949 Tactical and Technical characteristics – data furnished by Remdizel, with additional input from JSC Rosoboronexport

Wheel formula: 4x4
Engine: 610.10.350 (Cummins 6ISBe 350 P-6) (Rosoboronexport))
Engine power, maximum: 257.4 kW (350 hp.)
Maximum engine torque: 1078 Nm (110 kgf) (Rosoboronexport states 1090 Nm and 109 kgfm)
Fuel type: diesel
Transmission: automatic
Suspension: independent
Fuel tanks, number and capacity: two tanks, each with a capacity of 180 litres for a combined capacity of 360 litres
Vehicle curb weight: 14000 kg
Vehicle gross weight: 16000 kg
Power to weight ratio: 20.2 hp./ton
Length: 6370 mm
Width: 2550 mm
Height: 2960 mm
Ground clearance: 433 mm (adjustable)
Angle of non-overcome lift by car: at least 60%
Personnel capacity: 10
Transmission: automatic/9-speed sync, with drive cable and servo amplifier
Wheels: 10.00-20 (Rosoboronexport states 10.00-10)
Tires: 14.00 R20
Gradient: 31°
Fording depth: 1.5 m without preparation and 1.75 m with preparation
Horizontal obstacle (trench) overcome: 0.5 m
Vertical obstacle overcome: 0.6 m
Cruise range: at least 1000 km
Maximum speed: 105 km/h (Rosoboronexport states 100 km/h)
Vehicle electrical system power: 24 V

TYPHOON K-53949 medical module – The Typhoon K-53949 chassis formed the basis for the 'Lens' (medical) armoured vehicle, developed specifically for the MODRF. This variant, developed jointly by the respective design bureau and the medical service of the MODRF, featured a double cabin in place of the single cabin of the standard K-53949 (Remdizel).

The K-53949 medical module is tasked with medical support/evacuation. The variant is available in two sub-versions – 7+2 and 3+2 capacity – dependent on requirements. The vehicles are intended for, and equipped for, the location of wounded personnel and for the rendering of immediate medical assistance, either outside or inside the vehicle (Remdizel).

Previous page top: Typhoon K-53949. Previous page bottom and this page: Typhoon K-53949 medical module. MODRF/Remdizel

In the second decade of the twenty first century, the Russian Federation ground forces underwent extensive planning and implementation toward development of 50 medical companies for provision of medical assistance from initial response to surgery. Planning called for modernisation and re-equipment of medical transport assets. This included plans to acquire medical configured aircraft – 2 Il-76MD Scalpel-MT evacuation/resuscitation aircraft, 6 evacuation/resuscitation aircraft developed from the Il-112V or An-148 and a fleet of 12 Russian Helicopters Mi-8MTV-5 medium helicopters. The ground transport element was to be met by various platforms that were dropped, opening the door for acquisition of the Typhoon K-53949 medical module. The ground medical transport acquisition was intended to replace the relatively primitive LuAZ-967 (small size vehicle with amphibious capability, designed to evacuate injured personnel from the immediate hazard zone) and the UAZ-3962 'Loaf', effectively a road ambulance unsuited for evacuating injured personnel from a rough terrain environment. This later vehicle was to have been replaced by the UAZ-3972 (basically a road ambulance with limited rough terrain capability), but this program and another potential replacement, the UAZ-2970 (a road ambulance with limited rough terrain capability), was not brought to fruition. When these designs proved unsuitable for operational needs, evaluations were conducted into the practicality and suitability of battlefield medical evacuation designs based on the Kamaz-4350I chassis, designated AC4350 and AC4350I respectively, and Ural-43206 chassis. However, these platforms, although possessing good rough terrain capability, were not acceptable as they did not provision comfortable transportation of casualties and lacked armour protection. For high intensity combat operations, the Russian ground forces employed the BMP (tracked) and BTR (wheeled) armoured vehicles for casualty evacuation. In regard to the BMP-1 chassis, this included the BMM-1, BMM-2 and BMM-3, along with the BMD-D, whilst the BRT-MD was employed by Soviet and later Russian Federation airborne units. Another medical evacuation asset was present in the MT-LB armoured personnel carrier (not outfitted as a medical evacuation platform, but employed as such in both Chechen wars). This tracked vehicle is an old design (MT-LB is undergoing update at Remdizel) and not available in adequate numbers. The lack of modern battlefield medical evacuation vehicles led to development of the BMM-80 'Symphony' based on the GAZ-59039 chassis. Although a small number of such armoured vehicles were acquired, they did not enter mass production.

In 2016, the MODRF issued two tender contracts for development of armoured medical evacuation vehicles. The 'Kurganets-M' was to be developed from the BMP-3 – two variants, BMM-K1 armoured medical transport vehicle and BMM-K2 armoured medical center. The status of this program is uncertain in late 2019, and may have been cancelled. The contract for development of a medical vehicle that led to Typhoon K-53949 medical module was revealed in September 2016. Development of this secure tactical ambulance platform – to be based on the Typhoon K-53949 or the Tigr-M armoured vehicles – initiated under the code name 'Lens', was to be completed by 30 November 2017 (Remdizel).

The K-53949 medical module is available in two variants – ZSA-T & ZSA-P. The ZSA-T medical transporter is intended for location and retrieval of injured personnel. Capacity is three crew and six passengers on folding seats. When the seats are folded away the vehicle can accommodate 2-4 stretchers. The second configuration, ZSA-P, for equipping battalion level medical centres, is configured with five seats for the crew (including medical personnel) and provision for accommodation of two stretchers (Remdizel).

The Typhoon K-53949 medical modules, and Tigr M based medical module developments were initially rejected, resulting in a resubmission process in which the K-53949 emerged victorious. The prototype vehicles had been built and delivered during 2017, and a contract was awarded in 2018 for a batch of 27 Typhoon K-53949 medical modules for the Ministry of Defence of the Russian Federation. Delivery was to be effected during the 2019-2020 timeframe. The two variants, ZSA-T & ZSA-P, were re-designated ZA-53949A (medical conveyor) and ZSA-53949 (battalion level medical station) respectively in 2019.

Typhoon ZA-53949A medical conveyor/ZSA-53949 battalion level medical station tactical and technical characteristics – data furnished by Remdizel

Wheel formula: 4x4
Engine: 610.10.350 (Cummins 6ISBe 350 P-6)
Engine power, maximum: 257.4 kW (350 hp.)
Maximum engine torque: 1078 Nm (110 kgfm)
Fuel type: diesel
Fuel tanks, number and capacity: two tanks, each with a capacity of 180 litres for a combined capacity of 360 litres
Vehicle curb weight: 15000 kg
Vehicle gross weight: 16000 kg
Length: 7130 mm
Width: 2550 mm
Height: 3100 mm
Ground clearance: 433 mm (adjustable)
Personnel capacity: two versions – ZSA-T, two crew plus seven passengers (passengers can include includes 1 additional medical attendant). ZSA-P, 2 crew plus three passengers. Variations depend on whether the injured personnel are sitting or stretcher-borne
Transmission: sync cable-operated and servo amplified gears, 4-speed gearbox with reduction gear and planetary multiplier transmission
Wheels: 10.00-20
Tires: 14.00 R20
Cruise range: at least 1000 km
Maximum speed: 105 km/h

ТАЙФУН К-4386
ПОВЫШЕННАЯ ПРОХОДИМОСТЬ

TYPHOON K-4386 – The Typhoon K-4386 4x4 (often erroneously referred to as the Typhoon D) (the MODRF and Remdizel retain the Typhoon K designation) is a frameless vehicle capable of operating over rough, non-urban terrain. Like all members of the Typhoon K/U families the K-4386 is armoured to protect the crew from land mine/IED blasts and small arms or heavy machine gun fire up to 14.5 mm calibre (Remdizel).

The K-4386 was designed to equip the airborne forces of the Russian Federation, to which end it can be parachute dropped (Remdizel). In effect the K-4386 is a scaled down vehicle developed from the K-53949, designed as a fast armoured vehicle complementing the heavier armed BMD-4M tracked armoured personnel carrier in the Russian airborne forces. It has certain advantages over the larger/heavier variants of the Typhoon K. This includes increased maximum speed and increased maximum range. The second of these characteristic traits is of particular importance when operating in a tactical scenario in which resupply of fuel is problematic.

Typhoon K-4386 (left of photograph) was developed as a smaller, lighter 4x4 development based on the Typhoon K-53949 (right of photograph) for service with Russian airborne forces. Remdizel

The K-4386 has the lowest centre of mass and lowest overall mass of any Typhoon variant, enhancing the vehicles ability to traverse rough terrain. The design has three doors and features a similar independent spring suspension system to that installed on the K-53949. As is the case with the other members of the Typhoon K family, the K-4386 can operate at altitudes ranging from sea level up to 4500 m (Remdizel).

TYPHOON K

Page 57-58: Typhoon K-4386 during trials. Remdizel

The K-4386 is endowed with the same level of mine/IED blast and small arms/artillery ballistic protection of OTT Class 3 and OTT Class 4 as the K-63968 and K-53949. The design incorporates the 6.75 ton load self-extracting winch, a towing capability, fire extinguishing system, all-round camera system, and adds strobe lighting and an assault ladder. The communications suite incorporates a microwave communication system. The electronic systems can be powered by a combined electrical complex with an output of 24 V (Remdizel).

The combat module developed for the K-4386 – a derivative of the 32V01 uninhabited turret designed by CRI Burevestnik – is armed with a 30 mm calibre 2A42 automatic gun and a 7.62 mm calibre 6P7K machine gun. Ammunition capacity is 200 HE 30 mm, 100, AP-T 30 mm and 1,000 7.62 mm rounds. The turret, which weighs around 1.4 tons, is mounted on a bore with a diameter of 1350 mm and can traverse 360°, with an elevation for armament of -10° to +60°. The sighting complex consists of television and target indicator with laser rangefinder (CRI Burevestnik).

32V01 Combat Module – data furnished by CRI Burevestnik

Primary armament: 30 mm 2A42 automatic gun
Secondary armament: 7.62 mm 6P7K machine gun
Sight: TV and target indicator with integrated laser rangefinder
Engagement range: up to 4 km for the 2A42 automatic gun
Engagement range: up to 1.5 km for the 6P7K machine gun
Elevation angle: -10° to +60°
Traverse angle: 360°
2A42 automatic gun ammunition capacity: 200 30 mm HE rounds and 100 30 mm AP-T armour piercing rounds
6P7K machine gun ammunition capacity: 1000 7.62/54 mm rounds
32V01 module weight (including ammunition): no more than 1.5 ton
Module mounting bore: 1350 mm

The NPPU-80 2A42-1 30 mm rapid fire gun unit is capable of automatic and single shot firing. This weapon, is also incorporated in a number of wheeled and tracked armoured vehicles and Ka-52/K and Mi-28N attack helicopter. The unit employs a single-barrel gas operated action system to achieve high reliability in operation. A fixed receiver aids the ammunition belt feed, the ammunition being used up in a process of selective feeding, with alteration of firing rates. Extended close range firing is aided by the guns long barrel design, with significant enhancements to overall accuracy facilitated by the muzzle brake system and shock absorption of the recoiling barrel. This provides a steady firing platform by reducing oscillation of the mount at the exact instant each round is discharged (Tulamashzavod).

Typhoon K equipped with a 32V01 combat module (top) and a derived module (above). CRI Burevestnik

NPPU-80 2A42 30 mm rapid fire gun unit – data furnished by Tulamashzavod Production Association

Caliber: 30 mm
Weight of gun: 115 kg
Length of gun: 3027 mm
Rate of fire: 550-800 rounds per minute (high) or 200-300 rounds per minute (low)
Muzzle velocity: 960 m/s
Practicable range: up to 1500 m against lightly armoured targets and up to 4000 m against soft skinned targets
Recoil force: 40-50 kN (4000-5000 kgf)
DC power supply voltage of electric trigger and contractor: 27V
Gun ammunition feed: two-belt
Charging: pyrotechnic and manual
Firing control: remote from electric trigger and mechanical
Operating temperatures: ±50° centigrade

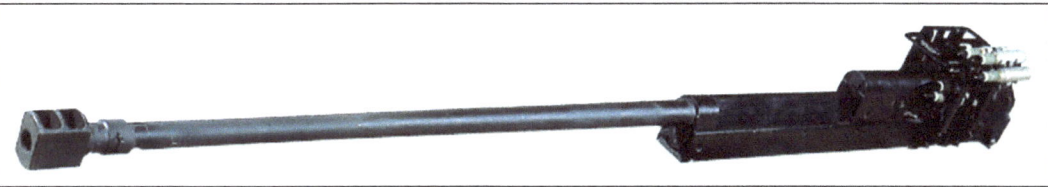

Typhoon K-4386 with 30 m cannon armed turret (above) and 2A42 30 mm automatic cannon (top). Remdizel/Tulamashzavod

The K-4386 has been demonstrated by CRI Burevestnik armed with what appears to be a breach loading mortar complex of undetermined calibre. This is housed in a turret complex alongside a 6S21 01 combat module (CRI Burevestnik). This would provide fire support to airborne troops when support by heavier weaponry is not available.

Top: Typhoon K-4386 shown during trials configured with what appears to be a turret mounted breach loading mortar complex and a 6S21 combat module. Above: K-4383 during trials. CRI Burevestnik/Remdizel

> Typhoon K-4386 Tactical and Technical Characteristics – Remdizel
>
> Wheel formula: 4x4
> Engine: 610.10.350
> Engine power, maximum: 257.4 kW (350 hp.)
> Maximum engine torque: 1078 Nm (110 kgfm)
> Fuel tanks, capacity and fuel type: one tank with a capacity of 200 litres of diesel
> Weights: curb, 11000 kg; gross, 13500 kg
> Dimensions: length, 6000 mm; width, 2544 mm; height, 2960 mm
> Ground clearance: 420 mm (adjustable)
> Personnel capacity: 7
> Transmission: sync, with a cable drive and servo amplifier with the inclusion of transfers. Planetary gearbox is installed in rear of main gearbox
> Wheels: 10.00-20
> Tires: 14.00 R20
> Cruise range: 1200 km
> Maximum speed: 130 km/h

The K-4386 has been developed into the 'Sketch' self-propelled 82 mm mortar carrier, unveiled in 2019, and an artillery fire control vehicle developed in cooperation with the Penza Research and Production [Development] enterprise, Rubin (either of these may refer to the development thought to be a breach loading mortar complex, noted above). A mobile mine carrier platform has also been developed (Remdizel). Conflicting information suggests that this is based on the K-53949 or K-4386 platforms. A tactical reconnaissance variant of the K-4386, designated MTP-K, was demonstrated at Prudboy proving ground, Volgograd region, Russia, at the end of May 2019 (MODRF).

A small batch of Typhoon K-4386 was modified as air defence platforms in cooperation with JSC Izhevsk Electromechanical Plant (Enterprise), Kupol – associated with OSA and Tor-M1 air defence missile systems (Izhevsk). This platform, referred to as the Typhoon-Air-Defence Vehicle, is armed with Igla MANPADS (Man-Portable Air Defence System). The Typhoon-Air-Defence Vehicle was designed and built in four months, primarily for participation in the Clear Skies 2019 air defence competition hosted in the Peoples Republic of China (competing against BTR-80 wheeled armoured vehicles armed with Igla MANPADS) (Press Service of the Southern Military District, 2019). Igla-S surface to air missiles can engage head-on airborne targets flying at up to 400 m/s and receding targets moving at up to 350 m/s at altitudes from 10-3500 m at ranges out to 6000 m (Rosoboronexport). It is unclear (in the first quarter of 2020) if the Typhoon-Air-Defence Vehicle is intended for service with the Russian airborne forces.

Trials of the baseline K4386 were completed in late 2018 or early 2019, paving the way for series production and delivery to units of the Russian airborne forces (Remdizel & MODRF).

Typhoon K-4386 MTP-K tactical reconnaissance platform, Prudboy proving ground, Volgograd region, Russia, circa 31 May 2019 (page 64 top) and Typhoon-Air Defence Vehicle during MODRF trials, circa 26 May 2019 (page 64 bottom and this page). MODRF

Typhoon-Air Defence Vehicle (Page 66 top). Typhoon-Air Defence Vehicle participated in the Army Inter Games-2019 at Korla proving ground, Peoples Republic of China, circa 31 July 2019 (page 67). Typhoon-Air Defence Vehicle competed against BTR armoured vehicles armed with Igla MANPADS – Russian Baltic Fleet represented in February 2019 (page 66 bottom). MODRF

Typhoon K-63968 during trials (top) and Typhoon K-63968 delivered to specialist forces division of the Russian WMD, circa 18 October 2016 (above). Remdizel/MODRF

Remdizel states that there are no plans to develop new variations of the K-63968, although there are musings at the idea of fitting some vehicles out for the communications/command role (Remdizel). New variants of the K-53949 include a de-mining vehicle and a reconnaissance/surveillance variant (Remdizel).

Gibka-S air defense complex based on the Tigr M 4x4 vehicle. This may indicate a potential layout for further evolution (conjectured) of the K-4386, based on the Typhoon-Air Defence Vehicle. Various wheeled and tracked vehicles, including Typhoon K-63968 and K-53949 in June 2019 (above). NPOVK/MODRF

Top: Specialist forces of the Russian SMD conduct driving training in adverse field conditions circa mid-December 2016. Bottom: Typhoon K-63968 of the Russian SMD in the Kuban, circa June 2018. MODRF

TYPHOON K

Top: Typhoon K-63968. MODRF documentation suggests that it is from the Russian CMD, Samara Region. Bottom: Typhoon K-63968 during field maneuver. MODRF

Top: Russian road convoy headed by a Tigr M armoured car trailed by a Typhoon K-63968, 2019. Bottom: MODRF documentation suggests that this Typhoon K-63968 is operating with a specialist force unit in Siberia, 2018. MODRF

Top: MODRF documentation suggests that this Typhoon K-63968 is operating with a specialist force unit of the CMD, Novosibirsk Region, circa April 2018. Above: Typhoon K-63868 being transported across a river obstacle by a PMM-2M ferry-bridge platform in July 2019. MODRF

While the primary Typhoon K customer was the Russian Federation ground forces, in 2019 the K-63969 and K-53949 were being marketed for foreign sale (Rosoboronexport), but the K-63968 and K-4386 were not actively marketed for foreign sale. The latter is intended for airborne forces and may be held back to push the K-53949 and the smaller Tigr and Lynx armoured car series to the fore. The K-63968 may be pushed for export once the bulk of Russian domestic demand has been met.

An early recipient of Typhoon K-63968 was Russian ground forces specialist units in the Rostov region, Krasnodar and Stavropol territories of the SMD (Southern Military District) These units received around 60 such vehicles by the end of 2013/early 2014 (Press Service of the Southern Military District, 2013). Typhoon K-63968 platforms were delivered to units in the SMD through 2014, with around 30 delivered around 25 December 2014 (Press Service of the Southern Military District, 2014) with deliveries continuing through the first quarter of 2015 (Press Service of the Southern Military District, 2015). Other Russian military districts were increasingly equipped with Typhoon K through the second half of the second decade of the twenty first century. A batch of 15 Typhoon K-63968 vehicles entered service with a reconnaissance unit in the Nizhny-Novgorod region of the WMD (ZVO) (Western Military District) circa end of November/early December 2016, followed by a batch of K-63968 delivered to a specialist force brigade of the WDM around 21 December 2016 (Press Service of the Western Military District, 2016). Typhoon K (apparently K-63968) entered service with a reconnaissance unit of the WMD, when eight such vehicles were delivered around 22 April 2017 (Press Service of the Western Military District, 2017). A batch of 16 Typhoon K, apparently K-63968, equipped with the Arbalet-DM combat module, were delivered to a specialist force unit based in the Samara and Novosibirsk regions of the CMD (Central Military District) around 22 December 2017 (Press Service of the Central Military District, 2017). A batch of eight K-63968 vehicles was delivered to a unit in the Novosibirsk region of the CMD around 9 April 2018 (Press Service of the Central Military District, 2018).

Russian CMD specialist force units ramped up training on K-53949 vehicles toward the end of May 2018, having participated in a military exercise at the Shilovo training range in the Novosibirsk area at the end of April that year. Eight K-53949 vehicles had been delivered in the first half of April (Press Service of the Central Military District, 2018). This exercise, which focused on anti-ambush drills, also involved units operating K-63968 and Tigr M armoured vehicles. Typhoon K-63968 vehicles entered service (six vehicles) with specialist force units in Siberia around 1 June 2018 (Press Service of the Central Military District, 2018).

Total Typhoon K numbers to be procured under MODRF contracts remained classified at December 2019, but the numbers delivered up to that time was certainly in the hundreds, with deliveries continuing in 2020. The K-63938 and K-53949 vehicles have been deployed for operations in the Syrian Arab Republic (MODRF & Remdizel) where they are employed on Russian base defence as well as patrols of areas liberated from Islamic State and other extremist groups.

Russian Federation victory parade at Hmeymim (Khmeimin) air base, Syria, 7 May 2019, celebrating victory in Europe in World War II. A Typhoon K-53949 leads a pair of Typhoon K-63968 vehicles. In the background are various assets of the Russian air group deployed to Syria, including Sukhoi Su-34, S-35S and Su-30SM multifunctional strike fighters MODRF

Top: MODRF data suggests that this Typhoon K-63968, in blustery snow conditions, was operating with a unit of the SMD in 2015. Bottom: A Typhoon K-63968 operating in winter conditions in the Siberian Steppe. MODRF

Quartet of Typhoon K-63968 of a unit of the CMD trails a Tigr M armoured vehicle in the Samara region of Russia in July 2019 (top) and Typhoon K-63968 & Tigr M vehicles during a field exercise near Novosibirsk in the Russian SMD in April 2018. MODRF

GLOSSARY

API	Armour Piercing Incendiary
ATGM	Anti-Tank Guided Missile
CMD	Central Military District
Cold War	Period of heightened tension and military stand-off between the power blocks of East and West, typically considered to have commenced circa 1947 and ended in the early 1990's
CRI	Central Research Institute
dB	Decibel
g	Gram
GLONASS	Globanaya Navigozionnaya Sputnikovaya Sistema (Global Navigation Satellite System)
GPS	Global Positioning System
HE	High Explosive
HEAT	High Explosive Anti-Tank
HF	High Frequency
IED	Improvised Explosive Device
IFV	Infantry Fighting Vehicle
JSC	Joint Stock Company
K	KamAZ
kg	Kilogram
km	Kilometre
km/h	Kilometres per hour
kW	Kilowatt
m	Metre
MANPADS	Man-Portable Air Defence System
MBT	Main Battle Tank
MHz	Megahertz
mm	Millimetre
MODRF	Ministry of Defence of the Russian Federation
MRAP	Mine Resistant Ambush Protected
m/s	Metres per second
mW	Megawatt
NATO	North Atlantic Treaty Organisation
OJSC	Open Joint Stock Company
rpm	Rounds Per Minute

SMD	Southern Military District
Soviet Union	Union of Soviet Socialist Republics (dissolved on 25 December 1991 and replaced with a Commonwealth of Independent States, with the Russian Federation as the main successor state)
TNT	Trinitrotoluene – a high explosive chemical formation
TV	Television
TV/IR	Television/Infrared
U	Ural
UAV	Uninhabited Air Vehicle
VHF	Very High Frequency
Victory Day parade	Event held annually in the Russian Federation to mark victory in Europe in May 1945
W	Watt
WMD	Western Military District
°	Degree(s)
±	Plus or minus
x	Times, multiplication
~	Approximately equal to (can also be used to mean asymptotically equal)

ABOUT THE AUTHOR

Hugh Harkins FRAS is a geophysicist/historian and author with an extensive research/study background in aeronautic, astronautic, astrophysics, nautical and the wider scientific, technical and historical fields. He is also involved in research in the field of Scottish history, which formed significant elements of dual undergraduate degrees. Hugh has published in excess of sixty books, non-fiction and fiction, writing under his given name as well as utilising several pseudonyms. He has also written for several international magazines, whilst his work has been used as reference for many other projects, ranging from the aviation industry, international news corporations and film media to encyclopaedias, museum exhibits and the computer gaming industry. Hugh is a member of the Institute of Physics and is an elected Fellow of the Royal Astronomical Society. He currently resides in his native Scotland.

Other titles by the author include:

Russia's Coastal Missile Shield - Bal-E & Bastion Mobile Coastal Cruise Missile Complexes
Iskander - Mobile Tactical Aero-Ballistic/Cruise Missile Complex
Orbital/Fractional Orbit Bombardment System - The Soviet Globalnaya Raketa
Counter-Space Defence Co-Orbital Satellite Fighter
Russia's Strategic Missile Carrier/Bomber Roadmap 2018-2040 – PAK DA, Tu-160M2, Tu-95MSM & Tu-22M3M
Sukhoi T-50/PAK FA - Russia's 5th Generation 'Stealth' Fighter
Sukhoi Su-35S 'Flanker' E - Russia's 4++ Generation Super-Manoeuvrability Fighter
Sukhoi Su-30MKK/MK2/M2 - Russo Kitashiy Striker from Amur
MiG-35/D 'Fulcrum' F – Towards the Fifth Generation
Air War over Syria, Tu-160, Tu-95MS & Tu-22M3 - Cruise Missile and Bombing Strikes on Syria, November 2015-February 2016
Sukhoi Su-27SM(3)/SKM
Russian/Soviet Aircraft Carrier & Carrier Aviation Design & Evolution Volume 1 - Seaplane Carriers, Project 71/72, Graf Zeppelin, Project 1123 ASW Cruiser & Project 1143-1143.4 Heavy Aircraft Carrying Cruiser
Soviet Mixed Power Experimental Fighter Aircraft – Piston-Liquid Propellant Rocket Engine/Piston-Ramjet/Piston-Pulsejet & Piston-Compressor Jet Engine Designs of the 1940's
Raid on the Forth - The First German Air Raid on Great Britain in World War II
The Battle of Kilsyth, 15 August 1645 - Montrose Baillie and The Keys to Scotland
Light Battle Cruisers and the Second Battle of Heligoland Bight
Into The Cauldron - The Lancaster MK.I Daylight Raid on Augsburg
Hurricane IIB Combat Log - 151 Wing RAF, North Russia 1941
RAF Meteor Jet Fighters in World War II, an Operational Log
Typhoon IA/B Combat Log - Operation Jubilee, August 1942
Defiant MK.I Combat Log - Fighter Command, May-September 1940
Blenheim MK.IF Combat Log - Fighter Command Day Fighter Sweeps/Night Interceptions, September 1939 - June 1940
Fortress MK.I Combat Log - Bomber Command High Altitude Bombing Operations, July-September 1941
Light Battle Cruisers and the Second Battle of Heligoland Bight
British Battlecruisers of World War 1 - Operational Log, July 1914-June 1915
Eurofighter Typhoon - Storm over Europe
North American F-108 Rapier - Mach 3 Interceptor
Convair YB-60 - Fort Worth Overcast
Boeing X-36 Tailless Agility Flight Research Aircraft
X-32 - The Boeing Joint Strike Fighter

www.ingramcontent.com/pod-product-compliance
Lightning Source LLC
Chambersburg PA
CBHW042012150426
43195CB00003B/99